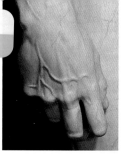

Readings and itineraries
4

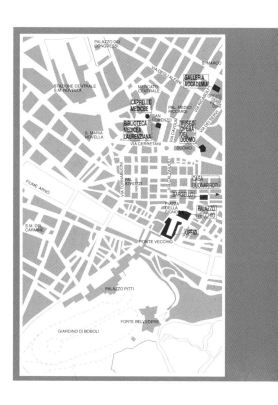

On page 3:
Furia, ca. 1525, GDSU
On page 62:
Venus, Mars and Cupid, ca. 1530, GDSU
Model for the *Tomb of Julius II*, GDSU
On page 64:
Sketch of an Apostle, GDSU

A publication of
s i l l a b e s.r.l.
Livorno

www.sillabe.it

managing editor: *Maddalena Paola Winspeare*
graphic design: *Laura Belforte*
translation: *Anthony Cafazzo*
editing: *Bettina Müller*

reproduction rights:
Archivio Casa Buonarroti; Archivio GDSU; Archivio Mandragora; Archivio sillabe: foto Paolo Nannoni; Nicolò Orsi Battaglini
The photographs of the Medici-Laurentian Library have been kindly furnished by its management

ISBN 978-88-8347-029-5

printed by Media Print. Livorno

Reprint	Year
5 6 7 8 9 10 11 12	2017 2018 2019 2020 2021 2022 2023 2024 2025

Raffaele Monti

Readings and itineraries

Michelangelo
Buonarroti

sillabe

Michelangelo in Florence

Marked by Michelangelo's genius in its very urban fabric, Florence even today offers a privileged path through the entire career of the greatest creator of new realities that the history of modern man has bequeathed us. Michelangelo Buonarroti succeeded in creating a new language all his own, a language with which he would ultimately foster a renewed awareness of the values and innovative abilities of Man himself.

Forgive me these, perhaps redundant lines that I felt compelled to set down because it seems that just recently the musings of specialised critics – naturally with well known exceptions – have attempted to reduce this phenomenal act of self-awareness, arrived at through the identification of form with the 'human', to an attributive rebus or rhetorical theme.

We shall therefore strive to discern a "michelangelesque path" through the complex and history-laden streets of Florence's city centre, so as to enable the visitor to retrace and comprehend to the fullest some of the fundamental stages of the work of this man endowed with an ethical consciousness and formal vision without precedent.

Fortunately, Florence, which was a "thankless land" for the artist, at least in many dramatic periods of its history, has preserved, even more than Rome (setting aside the objective *grandeur* of the Vatican frescoes), an extraordinary harvest of the sculptor's works. Beginning then with the Buonarroti family house in Via del Proconsolo, where some of the major sculptures from the artist's youth are preserved, then continuing through some of Florence's greatest museums, we shall conclude our reconnaissance with a contemplation of the Medici Chapels behind the church of San Lorenzo, Michelangelo's cardinal architectural-sculptural work (fortunately preserved absolutely intact), and an examination of the *Pietà,* the masterpiece of Michelangelo's last years, held in the Museum of the Opera del Duomo.

Opposite page:
*Transporting David
from Piazza della
Signoria to the Gallery
of the Accademia,*
from "Nuova
Illustrazione
Universale", 1874

4

Casa Buonarroti

Therefore, as mentioned, this exciting path through Florence, capable of re-establishing the definition of Michelangelo's art and its myriad facets, begins in the rooms of the Museum of Casa Buonarroti, housed in the buildings that once belonged to his brothers and descendants, and that already in the early 17th Century had become the cradle of the cult surrounding Michelangelo.

In effect, this unusual home *cum* museum, holds, apart from an important series of drawings, some of the fundamental works from Michelangelo's early years, two of which have been documented with certainty: the so-called *Madonna of the Steps* and the *Battle of the Centaurs*.

The former of these two marbles is mentioned by Vasari as Michelangelo's first sculptural work. The bas-relief, in fact, offered this historian-artist from Arezzo the occasion to set forth the first of his many *exemplas* devoted to Michelangelo in his *Lives of the Most Eminent Painters, Sculptors and Architects*, to demonstrate Michelangelo's ability to achieve anything he put his mind to, which in this specific case: "in seeking to imitate Donatello's style, his execution was so perfect that it seemed to have been done by his very hand, except for the visibly greater grace and better drawing". The work was given by Leonardo Buonarroti to Francesco de' Medici and returned to the Buonarroti family by the grand duke Cosimo II in 1617.

It is therefore quite remarkable that despite such truly distinguished testimonies to the work's authenticity, some critics have nonetheless put the small bas-relief's authorship in doubt and indicated various dates for its execution. According to the latest expert opinions, the work, fully recognised as the *Maestro's*, was performed around 1490, therefore in the years of his full maturity. In fact, the similarity in style to the work of Donatello of which Vasari speaks is clear especially in the spatial design that exploits the steep depth effects of the "stiacciato" style to define a space of extraordinary breadth within which the dynamic

Madonna of the Steps, ca. 1490

figures of the children can unfold. The work also shows evident similarities in iconography and spatial blending with Donatello's *Herod's Banquet*, today in the Musée des Beaux Arts in Lille. This small Madonna, the direct consequence of that fundamental exploration of space conceived of as dramatic rationality (according to the consummate study that Donatello, following Masaccio's example, conducted in his *Trinità* of Santa Maria Novella) unequivocally indicates the dominant theme which would underlie all of Michelangelo's formal designs. It is an early sign, but nonetheless so clear-cut and exacting as to stupefy all who manage to realise its precision.

Although the structural measure, based on multiplying the volume of the low step where the Madonna is seated, conforms to the metric canons of 15th-century Florentine art, the continuous overturning of these principles in points of high tension provides a telling indication of Michelangelo's desire to transcend the rules within their selfsame definitions – a process underlying the most complex works of this phase of the sculptor's formation.

Casa Buonarroti also houses the *Battle of the Centaurs*, a high relief that unfolds in at least three depth planes, in which Michelangelo, narrating an episode drawn from Ovid's *Metamorphoses*, seems to attempt an experimental fusion of his profound knowledge of and devotion to Donatello's late style, but also an uneasy, dramatic rereading of the gothic roots of Tuscan sculpture, especially Giovanni Pisano. The work, also datable to about 1490-1492, is performed through Michelangelo's "delving". That is, while carefully gauging the overall space available for its execution, he extracts the narrative elements from the raw material, often varying them according to the immediate demands of a not wholly formed plan, and often even ignores the anatomical 'errors' in some figures, which are not errors at all, but purposeful, dramatic, albeit unconventional, solutions. In fact, these 'errors' have always led this work to be deemed 'imperfect' – a judgement that neglects Michelangelo's unique interpreta-

Battle of the Centaurs,
1490-1492

Santo Spirito Crucifix,
1492-1493

tion of the concept of 'perfection' in the finishing of his works. In order to better understand this work, it should be noted how the young artist freely measures the depths by highly polishing the projecting surfaces and broadening the meshwork of background light, through a method very similar to his later, celebrated style of "non finito" (i.e., not-finished), as the planes extend back toward the distance, formed by scabrous surfaces, transparent and sensitive to light and its incidence. Reading the third sculpture found here, the so-called *Santo Spirito Crucifix,* poses rather thornier questions. Probably, by the time this book is available, this work, which is occasionally displayed in this same museum, will have been returned to the church whence it originated. Notwithstanding, we prefer to address it here, within the living core of Michelangelo's early activities. All historical sources speak of a wooden Crucifix performed by Michelangelo immediately after 1492 for the high altar of the church of Santo Spirito, in whose convent Michelangelo was allowed by the prior, Nicolao Bicchiellini, to furtively study anatomy on cadavers, a practice, as is well known, forbidden at the time. When the high altar was dismantled in the early 17th Century, and Giovan Battista Caccini built his masterpiece in its place, Michelangelo's crucifix was put in the convent's quarters and, implausibly, forgotten until 1962, when Margrit Lisner realised that it might be the Crucifix referred to in historical texts. Once restored, the work proved to be so complex and elaborated, even in its colouring, that many critics have come to agree, and justifiably so, that it is indeed the work of which Vasari and Condivi wrote.

The Museum of the Bargello

Near Casa Buonarroti, the so-called Museum of the Bargello is housed in what was once the Hall of Justice. Devoted mainly to sculpture, at least in its most spectacular core, it holds four masterpieces by Michelangelo, amongst which *Bacchus*, the first work to earn the sculptor renown and which scholarly tradition has always considered as defining the style of Michelangelo's mature years.

Condivi himself (Michelangelo's official biographer) recounts the complex history of this work, a history at once anomalous and paradigmatic, which is however obviously laced with fanciful and 'exemplifying' elements. Be that as it may, Condivi narrates how Michelangelo, just back from Bologna where he had finished the statuettes of the *Ark for the church of San Domenico*, left incomplete by Jacopo Della Quercia, sculpted a *Sleeping Cupid* and, at the suggestion of Lorenzo di Pierfrancesco de' Medici, treated it so as to make it appear ancient and had it sent to Rome, where it was sold as an 'antiquity' to the cardinal of San Giorgio. The deception was discovered by the cardinal, who in turn sold it to the duke Valentino (the misadventures of this marble and the numerous copies made of it constitute one of the most curious chapters in the history of artistic attribution). However, the cardinal spoke so well of the young artist's imitative talents that the Roman gentleman, Jacopo Galli, commissioned from him "... a marble Bacchus of ten palms height, whose form and aspect correspond in its every part to the intentions of ancient sculptors".

Today perhaps even the attentive spectator may miss this decisive aspiration to the classical, which seems to have offered Michelangelo the occasion to depart from the compositional tradition of late 15th-century Florence and especially the late style of Donatello, whose influence, as we have already seen, was fundamental in both the style and execution of the *Madonna of the Steps*.

To establish a clear vantage point from which to begin and develop the viewing of this *Bacchus*, Michelangelo forsakes the traditional frontal perspective which, perhaps following the example of Jacopo Della Quercia, he had already transcended in developing the varied profiles of the angel in the *Ark* in Bologna. He there-

Opposite page:
Bacchus, 1496-1497

10

fore imparts movement to the structure, above all through the realistic staggering on three interfering planes, whose concatenation is enhanced by the mobility of the incident light and point of view. These, in reality, are the truly innovative elements of the *Battle of the Centaurs* that we have just seen in Casa Buonarroti.

In *Bacchus* the space within which the figure unfolds becomes the fundamental, all-bearing element, in a dialectical tension between the 'material' defining the statuary form and the incipient movement that is just beginning, with a rapid start, in the uplifting of the right foot, and develops quickly, signalling the principal point of viewing, which, as we have mentioned above, changes continually in the multiplication and twisting of the forces coming to bear. In this way, the god's gesture reveals the complementary figure of the Satyr set at his feet and who seems bound to him in the interlacing of their bodies interrupted by the gnarl of Bacchus' hand holding the lion skin and cluster of grapes.

Yet it is this second figure, that, as we shall see, defines and resolves the work's narrative 'meaning'. The Satyr is completely masked by one's first perception of the figures which, as mentioned, begins with Bacchus' right foot, set toes down on the base, and then revolves through manifold perspectives, all linked by the coursing of the sculpted lines and twisting profiles, each independent in and of itself but acting to define the next view. As the eyes follow this twisting course, they finally come upon the small figure of the Satyr, almost hidden and sustaining the looming larger figure. From this moment, a renewed point of view reveals a preferential vision, tensed in the

perfect arc of the god's body and knotted in the centre by the hand upholding the fir, then interrupted by the long index finger. The eyes are then directed over the legs of the faun and held just barely by the rhythmic perfection of the structures behind, which through an extraordinary sense of vital tension leads the viewer's gaze over the right hip, up to the point whence the course originated, not terminating it, but providing the opportunity to contemplate the worked material (marble) and the space containing it.

Having concluded this reading, one understands exactly how the representation's meaning, even in its archaeological implications, defines a completely new value in the history of forms: it is an unheard-of process imparting new significance to the axiality of 15th-century Florentine sculpture, as interconnected and concatenated as it may have been. It is through this same stylistic process that Michelangelo reveals the work's symbolic and narrative meaning, eliminating the mediated interdependence in use until then. In fact, the evident metaphor expressed through the formal connotations (the decline of the drunken god, despite its occurring in a complex context of life force and impending death, as suggested by the lion's mask) go far beyond the simple narrative and symbolic characterisation dominant within the whole iconographic system in use up to then (even in the most piercing and problematic versions of Donatello and Jacopo Della Quercia), to become the compelling motive for language, the very reason for that something extra, both cognitive and emotional, that the artist defines through the pure means of form and vision.

In fact, in these same years, between the 15th and 16th Centuries, such aspects can be discerned in the works of other great Florentine formal masters, such as Leonardo da Vinci, despite the very different movement and tension he imparts, and even the mature Raphael, apart from his neo-platonic tendencies.

Such a way of identifying and unifying form with consciousness is the highest and, in a certain sense, the culminating event of a century of unbelievable cognitive and artistic conquests, which saw Florence and its figurative culture as the emerging motive centre of a way of re-valorising man's power to act in the face of history. From its heart in Tuscany a movement would then spread for the renewal man's self-awareness and his relation to the objects of knowledge and their creator, a movement that would influence Galileo and act as motive force at least up to the great intellectual crises of the late 17th and early 18th Centuries.

In fact, herein lies the grounds for the importance and absolutely unequalled fame attributed to these three artists even during their own lifetimes. It was they who identified the perfect and yet dramatic correspondence between form and human consciousness, indivisible elements in continual dialectical relation in their internal revelation.

Bacchus is perhaps the first finished example of this new totality in-

spired by Michelangelo. It is remarkable how the sculptor exploits memories of the past, yes, imposed by the buyer, but already present in the formidable historical re-examination he undertakes as his style develops and takes shape.

In concluding our brief examination of this fundamental work, we shall dwell on some as yet unclarified particulars in its 'history'. Many of the statues' details are in fact damaged, and the right hand holding the cup was evidently executed, rather more poorly, after the work had been complet-

ed. Other details are clearly lacking, such as the penis and almost all the parts in relief of the vine shoots crowning the god's head.

Regarding the sexual parts and hand, it is nearly certain that they were removed on purpose in order to impart the duly 'archaeological' appearance that the statue was supposed to have (the hand was subsequently reinserted under the supervision of the sculptor himself). The breaking off of the vine shoots instead seems to be due to real damage and ageing. In any event, this is still an open problem, especially considering that the leaves and shoots in relief would have completely altered the weight of the head and its equilibrium with the rest of the structure.

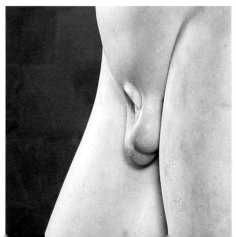

The superb series of Michelangelo's works held by the Bargello Museum includes another sculpture from these same years, the artist's Florentine period, the *Pitti Tondo*, depicting the Madonna and Child with young Saint John, probably commissioned from him by Bartolomeo Pitti between 1504 and 1505. This *tondo* brings up the issue of Michelangelo's "not-finished" which we have already had occasion to speak of in the complex themes of the *Battle of the Centaurs* at Casa Buonarroti. Vasari was the first to inform us that the sculptor "drafted and did not finish" this work and the other, *Taddei Tondo*, today in the London Royal Academy.

Certainly, in comparison with the polish of coeval works such as the *Bruges Madonna* or the Vatican *Pietà*, the heavily non-uniform surface of this *tondo* seems to indicate that the work's progress was interrupted before the traditional conclusive stage in which the same state of finish is imparted even to the varying levels of the surface depths and reliefs. In reality, as in the case of da Vinci's *Adoration of the Magi*, this lack of finish endows the work with such complex formal significance as to legitimately call into doubt, especially in such problematic and innovative artists as these, whether we are dealing with a purely chance occurrence. In fact, in the distribution of the deep planes that determine its structure, the aspect of "not-finished" involves the left-hand background, with the small figure of Saint John, most heavily, and less so the full figure of Jesus and the cloth on Mary's left arm, to which it imparts an effect of luminous highlighting. The only area really brought to full finish is the Virgin's face, that is, the portion of the figure that protrudes most, and whose crowned hairstyle rises considerably beyond the upper boundaries of the marble *tondo*.

Her exquisite, strong-featured countenance, enclosed in an accentuated geometry defined above by the crown with the figure of the cherub, symbol of loftier knowledge, is the reference point of the composition's equilibrium and the point of both departure and arrival of the mobile axis around which rotates the sphere defined by the figures and the space they create. In fact, as would occur later with the *Doni Tondo*, here a whole series of structural and symbolic problems are at issue, which had already been hinted at in some of the *tondi* by Botticelli and Filippo Lippi. Michelangelo highlights the definition of a sphere, that is, a true, measurable space outside of and beyond the point of maximum protrusion of the figures. The symbolic sphere (the Divinity, Eternity, Perfection), therefore departs from the traditional framing 'in

*Madonna and
Child with young
Saint John
("Pitti Tondo"),
1504-1505*

a window' that generally cut off the major characters at the waist. The Virgin, in fact, is depicted nearly full length within the limits of the space, in a succession of angular and winding courses that recalls Raphael's *Madonna of the chair*, composed externally through the triangulation originally formulated by da Vinci. Mary's face, which seems to force the space outward before her just beyond the purely optical membrane that defines the sphericity of the emergence, is also the symbolic centre, as it garners, in her profound and almost painful gaze, the very essence

of the divine and human drama that originates in her. Child Jesus is therefore set in the background, in the deeper plane, and even more so John, the Precursor, in a perspective device that finds its justification precisely in that dialectic between form and meaning mentioned earlier. Thus, the "not-finished", as in many works from the artist's maturity and old age, appears to be an irreplaceable means for defining such spatial effects without the need to set precise perspective indices (as in the *Doni Tondo*), which would have required finishing. Such finishing, however, may have rendered difficult and problematic the direct extrusion of power and emotions that the chisel can evoke and intimate.

The other two works by Michelangelo preserved in the Museum of the Bargello were done during the years of his full maturity. The spectator is therefore forced to mentally account for a thirty-year gap between these and the former two works – years at the very heart of his career, that saw, amongst many other projects, his ideating of the *Sistine Chapel Ceiling* and a substantial part of the execution of the *Tomb of Julius II.* This latter, a grandiose monument that he is known to have redesigned several times and finally performed in a very much reduced version, can be considered to be the unifying thread through which, year after year, Michelangelo's studies would develop.

Dramatic and splendid testimonies remain of this Cyclopean task, ultimately forsworn: the numerous sketches and many statues, including the so-called *Prisoners* of the Museum of the Accademia which we will speak of in due course.

In chronological order, the first of the two Bargello works is *Apollo*, in all probability sculpted between 1530 and 1532, which Vasari tells us was done for Baccio Valori, the papal plenipotentiary to Florence and city Regent. Also from Vasari come the accounts that would give rise to the history, or perhaps, legend of this masterpiece. It seems, in fact, that after the siege of Florence and the return to power of the Medici family, Michelangelo's position vis-à-vis the Medici was seriously compromised for his having designed the fortifications for the Florentine Republic. Upon their re-entry to the city, however, Michelangelo received their pardon, along with that of the Medici pope, Clement VII, thanks in part to the mediation of Valori. This *Apollo* was therefore to be a token of the artist's gratitude, who for the occasion re-elaborated his draft of a David begun in 1523 for the Medici Chapel. In fact, in the inventory of the Medici collections compiled under Cosimo I, it is referred to as *David*.

Therefore, whether it be *David* or *Apollo*, (the second hypothesis seems more in keeping with the true inner study of "manifest beauty" that this marble elicits), the marble figure, from the pivoting of the right foot to the tension of the left arm raised in direct relation to the smooth curve of the hips and torso, defines a course termed *serpentinato* (that is, "serpentine", a prime stylistic and theoretical element in Michelangelo's later works), which, although already discernible in *Bacchus*, here comes to involve the entire body. The relations amongst the various views as one moves around the figure, perceiving its rhythmic patterns, represent the key to its reading. Thus, the sinuous motion is to be viewed both in depth, in the frontal view, and especially in the relationships amongst the various view points, the most important of which is from the rear, as it is here that the figure's extraordinary motif is revealed, even in the inclination and rapid, yet considered raising of the head.

This beautiful sculpture is also "not-finished". Apart from the meshed and scalloped working of the material's surface, rendering it sensitive to incident light, it also bears two well squared-off fragments of the original marble block on which the figure seems to lean as if against a tree. Therefore, viewing it from the left side, the relationship between the flexion of the right knee and the residual marble is so perfectly calibrated (the tensed calf emerging with all the strength of the rock from which it origi-

Preceding page:
David-Apollo,
1530-1532

21

nates) as to justify the hypothesis of an extremely precise and wilful "not-finished" (as always with Michelangelo).

The last marble in the splendid series held in this museum, *Brutus* – the only bust sculpted by Michelangelo according to traditional canons of Roman classical portraiture – also has a curious, though relatively hypothetical history. It was sculpted in Rome after the Medici's return to Florence at the bidding of the Florentine humanist in exile, Donato Giannotti, for Cardinal Ridolfi, a fellow exile. Tradition has it that the statue is a portrait of Lorenzino de' Medici, who in 1536 assassinated the corrupt Alessandro de' Medici, and that it therefore represents a sort of celebration of the freedom gained through the supreme sacrifice, that of man's own conscience.

The couplet engraved on the base "Dum Bruti effigiem sculptor de marmore ducit / in mentem sceleris venit et abstinuit", probably dictated by Donato Giannotti, complicates the sculpture's history, in that it comes from a dialogue with Michelangelo written in 1545 by Giannotti himself, and concerns the consideration owed to he who kills the oppressor.

In the dialogue, Michelangelo's ethical position, in its dialectical sophistication, remains slightly ambiguous. This sculpture, on the other hand, reveals such positive assertiveness as to render obvious the artist's desire to celebrate the supreme value of liberty, expressing, in the strong and saddened look of the figure (an idealised self-portrait of the sculptor), his disdain for traitors and liberticides.

In any event, as can be gathered from the couplet, the work was left incomplete and was partly finished by Tiberio Calcagni (mostly the folds of the robe). This masterpiece, which also has evident affinities with Donatello's *Niccolò da Uzzano*, in the tension imparted to the head through the accentuated physiognomy, represents a revolution in the tradition of Florentine portraiture, which was, however, poorly understood at the time: the composition and classical cut of the bust justify the intense delineation of the 'portrait'. The character's beautiful face is set in meditation of his own conscience; the tight lips and self-absorbed look, in a sort of self-scrutiny, uncover and accentuate the torsion of the neck and the strong definition of the face. What emerges is an 'ethical portrait' of telling beauty and incredibly romantic portent.

Victory
of Palazzo Vecchio

After exiting the Museum of the Bargello and before entering the Uffizi, where the *Doni Tondo* is held,
a visit to Palazzo Vecchio's Hall of the Five Hundred
allows us to admire one of Michelangelo's most
beautiful, yet least well-known marble sculptural groups.

The sculpture in question is the so-called
Victory (a naked youth standing over an el-
derly man crouching on the ground with
face extended forward), done between 1528
and 1534 and probably intended for the
Tomb of Julius II.

The anomaly and, at the same time, singularity
of this marble group reside especially in its accentuated symbolic-narrative significance and
the free, nearly audacious development of the
upper figure. The serpentine flow of the beautiful nude figure (expressing the relationship
of space to figure, already seen in the coeval
Apollo, to the extreme) stems directly from the
tenseness of the old man, whose facial frontal-
ity generates the axis defining the movement and
its degrees of freedom. The slight emphasis that the
sculptor imparts to the bust of the victorious nude
serves to create a strong sense of movement that
contrasts and bridles the compact and unmoving
mass of rock from which it originates. In the development of the michelangelesque style, this
work was to have enormous consequences, both
in the short-term, on the so-called Mannerists
(especially, Giambologna), as well as on the
works of the greatest sculptors of the 17th
Century, including Bernini. The work's finishing,
done after Michelangelo's death by some of his
followers, amongst whom Daniele da Volterra,
has not in the least compromised the remarkable features just pointed out.

23

The *Doni Tondo* of the Uffizi

Only a few metres from the Hall of the Five Hundred, in one of the rooms of the Uffizi Museum, hangs the *Doni Tondo*, Michelangelo's only known surviving painting on wood panel and testimony to his extraordinary skill as a painter.

Performed in all likelihood in 1507 for the wedding of Maddalena Strozzi and Agnolo Doni, the large panel represents a cross-roads in his artistic activities, at which the rich experiences of his fiery youth and the formidable intuitions of his maturing genius (and, in reality, the whole of the civilisation surrounding him, with it secular glories and the torments of its troublesome modernism) melded to determine a sort of supreme 'mandala', a complex and renewed form within which his awareness was to unfold.

The formal choice of the *tondo* was probably dictated in part by the wishes of those who commissioned it (a well-known Florentine custom called for giving a bithplate as a wedding gift to the bride and groom). However, there is another, more profound aspect to this choice: just as in two contemporary sculptures, the *Pitti Madonna* and the *Taddei Madonna*, Michelangelo seeks, through compositional elements and, perhaps, also the use of convex mirror projections (according to the Flemish perspective methods previously adopted by Botticelli which would become fundamental to the new metrics defined by Pontormo) to define a circular space in which to create a sphere – the symbol of eternity and perfection.

At the centre of this sphere he sets the Holy Family, composed according to the pyramidal scheme originated by Leonardo da Vinci.

Above and following page:

Holy Family with young Saint John ("Doni Tondo"), ca. 1507

24

Actually, the pyramid is particularly delineated by the strong three-dimensionality of Mary's figure, whose twisting body defines the centre of a sort of hexahedron, formed by the figure of Saint Joseph passing the Child Jesus into Mary's arms. In turn, the entire group is enclosed within a second hexahedron, demarcated by the wall on which the nude figures are set leaning before the vast but foreshortened landscape in the volet. Central to this recurrent circling is the Madonna's gesture, as she reaches behind for the triumphal figure of Jesus, crowned with a headband just as the victorious athletes of old. The motion of the figure is so active, and the consequent force so complex, that another gesture seems tacit in the image – Mary's giving up her son to humanity, which looks on immediately behind. However, through the strong scaling of the proportions (probably performed using the technique of mirror projection), the small figure of young Saint John to the right is interposed as intermediary between the world renewed by Christ's arrival and humanity *ante legem*. The rod in Jesus' left hand, apart from marking one of the main perspective axes, also performs the function of interceding between the hexahedron of rocks and the splendid nude figures of the pagan world. The background, which also contains some architectural elements under construction, is reduced nearly to a series of hints and vague indications of tension, capable of holding back space, not infinitely, but within the perfect confines of sphericity. Michelangelo's choice of colours is extremely selective and used wholly to the purpose of defining and developing the spatial volumes. The results, limpid, new tones, able to tinge the cloth with an effect of growing volume-luminescence, is termed "cangiantismo" (roughly, 'iridescence') – a technique that would be used often, albeit with different aims, by Andrea del Sarto and some of the so-called Mannerists, especially Pontormo.

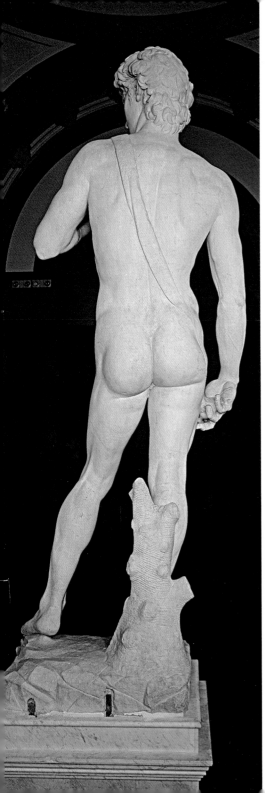

Another important Florentine museum, the Gallery of the Accademia, has the largest and most spectacular collection of Michelangelo's works in existence.

Instituted between the 18th and 19th Centuries by will of grand duke Pietro Leopoldo, the Gallery of the Accademia was destined to serve a 'pedagogical' function for students of the Academy of Arts and Drawing, the famous cultural and ideological institution founded by Vasari by order of the grand duke Cosimo I.

After the gallery's founding many paintings were transferred here from numerous other Florentine collections and churches. In 1873, the museum's holding were enriched by Michelangelo's *David*, which was removed from its original site in front of Palazzo Vecchio (and replaced with a good copy) because portions of the celebrated monument began to show decay due to the effects of the elements.

In 1882, the so-called *Tribuna* was completed, after the design of De Fabris. This is a large niche or apse at the back of the large open gallery, whose creation aimed to allow viewing the statue from a relatively distant vantage point. The new vaulted space proved to be quite functional and structurally suitable to reading the monument within a closed space, although Michelangelo himself had conceived it for exterior viewing and had it placed in piazza della Signoria, in a particularly significant spot where it would moreover establish a direct relationship with the massive looming structure of Palazzo Vecchio and its soaring tower.

In 1909 the Accademia received the four *Prisoners,* or *Slaves,* from the Buontalenti Grotto in Boboli Gardens, followed in 1939 by the so-called *Palestrina Pietà. Saint Matthew,* held in the Accademia since 1834, was also put on display in the Gallery. The six masterpieces were placed at the Gallery's sides, whose walls at the time were hung with precious tapestries. Thus, they are set, in all their magnetic grandeur, like milestones along an extraordinary path leading up to and culminating in the colossal *David*. The sight is an inspiring one and, given the exceptional quality of the individual works and the difficulty of reading them, admittedly represents one of the most suitable solutions ever found for exhibition of Michelangelo's masterpieces. In fact, this gallery, together with the rather more complex New Sacristy in San Lorenzo, is considered the heart of the cult of Michelangelo.

Upon entering, one is therefore immediately struck by David's vast dimensions, which the partitioning of the niche holding it, offering a free, unencumbered view, exalts within the gallery's space. In effect, Michelangelo – who sculpted the work not yet knowing where it would be placed – used such huge proportions, whose effect is further enhanced by the grandeur of the statue's turned head and intense gaze, in order to resolve the fundamental problem of the varying distance from which it would be viewed, especially regarding the monument's three outer sides (front and two lateral). The figure reveals a rapid movement which, beginning with the advancing left foot, ascends to culminate in the left hand holding the sling. Here, from a viewpoint shifted slightly to the right of the initial one, the hand appears wedged into the figure's chin, as if to discharge the enormous forces coursing through his entire body, precisely here, into the block of the head, terminating in the perfectly delineated features and hair.

Michelangelo sculpted this masterpiece on commission to the Opera del Duomo on a single block of marble – a sort of leftover from the workshops of the Opera del Duomo itself. It had initially been intended to decorate one of the outside buttresses of the church of Santa Maria del Fiore, then, at a later time (1463), it was consigned to Agostino di Duccio, who was to sculpt a gigantic nude, perhaps Hercules, David or some other subject. However, Agostino made little headway and had hardly begun work on the marble, when on August 18, 1501 it was finally entrusted to Michelangelo by the workers of the Opera del Duomo. Michelangelo was thereby bid to either finish the work or start it over from scratch. It was delivered in its present form precisely two years later. In 1504 a commission was formed that included Leonardo da Vinci, Botticelli, Perugino, Filippino Lippi and Piero di Cosimo to decide where to place this new colossus. It was thus decided to remove Donatello's *Judith* from its position just outside the front

Preceding page:
David, 1501-1504

door of Palazzo Vecchio and replace it with *David*. Such a position invested the representation with a new and stirring significance. David and Hercules were in fact the two figures that symbolised Florentine liberty — the former sacred, the latter symbolic-mythological — and the placement at the entrance to the "Palace of Lords" of such a *David* was therefore pregnant with extraordinary civil overtones. Some decades later, under quite different political circumstances, Bandinelli was to carry out the sculptural group of *Hercules and Cacus*, to serve as *pendant* to *David* on the other side of the entrance to Palazzo Vecchio.

Returning now to a reading of *David*, Michelangelo masterfully overcame the meagre depth of the block, which had originally been chosen by Agostino according to the canons of 15th-century statuary. The problem of developing the figure's depth in the block's limited thickness led the sculptor to truncate the carriage of the body in movement. In fact, the entire weight of the body is borne by the right leg, which extends along a perfect vertical plane formed by the fold of the arm and the leg itself, in a movement enhanced by the node defined by the large strong hand. The left side instead unfolds in a movement that spreads quickly onto the buttocks and torso whence it is 'discharged' onto the right shoulder. The head heightens and closes this sense of motion in progress.

There is an unprecedented *pathos* and yet a harmony defining this masterpiece that seem drawn from natural roots. Its perfection and the finish of its forms are not mere decorative qualities, but inner pulsings which, despite the statue's enormous proportions (avoided by other artists by now for centuries), bestow import to each and every detail. Perception of the proportions of and the tensions present in the magnificent head is not in the least altered by the statue's great height. In fact, Michelangelo actually accents the head to reiterate the strength of bearing and the formal and civic significance of this gigantic youth. Since its very first appearance, such significance was to be recognised and would contribute to creating the 'myth' of this *David* – a sculpture destined, over the centuries, to become the symbol of an epoch that would define many of the fundamentals of modern civilisation.

Immediately after completing *David*, Michelangelo began *Saint Matthew*, for which he had signed a contract in 1503 with the powerful "Arte della Lana" (Wool Guild) and which was to be the first of the twelve Apostles destined for the church of Santa Maria del Fiore. Called to Rome by the Pope in 1505, he was forced to suspend work, and the contract was rescinded at the end of the same year. Thus, *Saint Matthew*, property of the Opera del Duomo, remained in its current, embryonic state and in 1838 was brought to the Accademia delle Belle Arti.

As in the case of the four *Prisoners,* also in the Accademia, this statue's state of incompletion is evident and well-documented, and therefore not to be attributed to Michelangelo's "not-finished", which was a deliberate, formal choice. However, its very partialness invests this masterpiece with a particular aura, and as the other works just cited, reveals to us the very stages of elaboration of the new method that Michelangelo was developing – his delving into the marble to evoke, from the earliest stages, the flow and meaning of the entire figure. Even here, the overall plan of the image has been perfectly demarcated and one can clearly perceive the structural affinities with *David*, especially in the relationship between the right arm and leg, and accordingly, in the bipartite division (static right, dynamic left) which we have seen in the preceding statue. However, while wishing to avoid rhetoric, one cannot but underscore the more disconcerting quality of this masterpiece, interposed between idea and form in a transmutation-like state, by which the emotional

St. Matthew,
1505-1506

31

elements that would be excluded by surface finishing emerge in their pure state and fluctuate according to the incidence of the light, almost as if other, fleeting forms were concealed within the more obvious shape – forms just barely defined or still under development – forms that the variegated marks of the chisel disclose as in a true vision of inner movement.

The four sculptures that follow, the so-called *Prisoners*, have a complex history of their own and are, together with the *Slaves* in the Louvre, the most manifest testimony to the true drama of Michelangelo's long and arduous planning of the *Tomb of Julius II*. Michelangelo likely started these statues for the third version of his project for the tomb of the Pope in 1532. The *Prisoners* were to be placed, two on a side, beside the *Victory* group (today in

*Prisoners,
Young Slave,
ca. 1530*

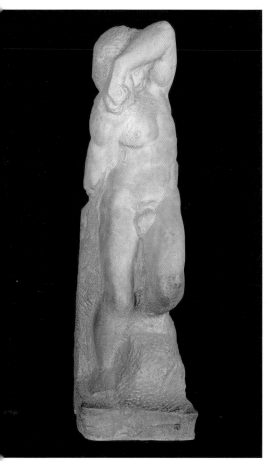

Palazzo Vecchio), a work that was to resolve, through a sort of painful liberation, the evident theme of slavery of the soul and the heroic limitations of the body.

Michelangelo probably worked on the four figures for quite a long time, at least the two years from 1530 to 1532. After the tomb's design was modified once again, the four marble blocks remained in Michelangelo's studio and in 1564 were sold by Leonardo Buonarroti, the sculptor's nephew, to Cosimo I, who entrusted them to Buontalenti, favourite architect of the Medici court. Buontalenti placed the four masterpieces in the famous Grotto that bears his name, a masterpiece of so-called Mannerist architecture which he built at the entrance to Boboli Gardens. In 1909 they were removed from the Grotto (and replaced with plaster casts) and set in the corridor of the Accademia.

Over the thirty years that the blocks of marble remained in the sculptor's studio in Rome, they represented a sort of ongoing, unconstrained creative point of reference for him, spurring him toward bold new artistic solutions. Thus, the hypothesis advanced by some that Buonarroti was totally indifferent to the work of developing their forms seems absurd. In fact, each statue clearly reveals Michelangelo's delving into the marble block "to raise", or draw forth the figure contained within. Moreover, the continuously varied chisel marks and, above all, the structural completeness unifying each figure, often complemented by the natural material itself, all suggest that Michelangelo, by now unencumbered by the requirements of the commission, could experiment freely and, therefore, purposely and precisely brought the four works to their actual states of completion (or rather, 'incompletion', the hallmark of his "not-finished").

In each of the statues, in fact, an intense relationship of forces is established between the emerging figure and the material-space enveloping and constraining it, while at the same time exalting the sense of tension.

The first, traditionally called the *Young Slave*, in both its movement and 'emotional state' seems to be linked to the so-called *Dying Slave* (today in the Louvre) performed between 1513 and 1516 for Michelangelo's first 'idea' for the tomb. Both these youthful prisoners seem to be awaking from an almost primordial sleep to stretch their fettered bodies. The relationship between the legs in the two statues is also very similar, while the gesture of the arm lifted to cover the face still partially encumbe-

Prisoners,
Reawakening Slave,
ca. 1530

33

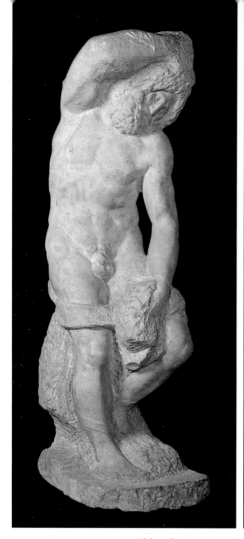

red by sleep seems, in the Florentine marble, to unfold at a time immediately prior that of the Slave in the Louvre. In fact, in this *Slave* of the Accademia, the nearly liberating gesture of its counterpart remains constrained within the material, and the face itself, only glimpsed behind the beautiful curve of the body, heightens the ambiguity of this state of dawning consciousness.

Even more dominated by the material engulfing it is the so-called *Reawakening Slave*, a hulking nude male depicted in the precise moment of his stirring. Rather, the creature envisaged by Michelangelo is represented in its primaeval stages, suspended at the irreproducible moment in which he liberates the figure "by

Below:
Prisoners,
Bearded Slave,

To the right:
Prisoners,
Atlas, ca. 1530

34

raising" it from the grip of tormenting stone and thereby disclos-
es it in its entirety, even its depths. The straining bust and bearded face seem to struggle to emerge from the stone, and the
movement of the legs, similar to, but a mirror image of that in the
following statue, bring us to the so-called *Bearded Slave*. This figure is more fully unveiled and free in space than the preceding
ones, even if all the compositional elements, from the tension in
the legs to the torsion of the bust, and the very position of the
arms almost seem to close the gnarl of the body, in direct reference to the fourth figure, the so-called *Atlas*. Here, the stone,
open at the right to release the forces of the upper block, closes
the figure above, where it preserves its rocky nature and renders
possible the "terrible" staggering of planes by which the an-
guished look of the man bearing an intolerable burden can be
glimpsed through the narrow fissure, almost bored through the
rock by the strength of his gaze itself, while the shadow thickens

around the left profile of his immense
body. The expressive power of these masterpieces is such that, in reading them, any
description of form must necessarily be
united with a revelation of contents. Thus,
any indications that may be provided on
the formal aspects are so evident and
meaningful that they may often seem mere
tautological emphasis. The last in this series is the so-called *Palestrina Pietà*, so
called because it reached the Medici collections from the Barberini Villa located in
Palestrina, near Rome. Although the work
certainly appears worthy of being attributed to Michelangelo, it is however the only one in the repertoire of Michelangelo
not to be documented from its origins,
and therefore not accepted by some critics as his work. And yet the strength of
synthesis of the three figures, the 'absolute' weight of Christ's body, sustained
by the immense hand of Mary and the
artist's skill in enclosing the three figures
within a single field of tension leave no
doubt about the work's authorship.

The Medici complex of San Lorenzo

The church of San Lorenzo and the structures surrounding it constitute a building complex whose individual parts are interdependent, yet characterised by their own extraordinary historical and artistic significance. Although the history of this unique site is too well known and complex to be taken up here in all its details, a brief summary seems in order. The original church was consecrated in the year 393 by the Bishop of Milan, Saint Ambrose. Then beginning in 1418, when Giovanni de' Bicci was commissioned by the Medici to enlarge it, the church came to represent the privileged place of worship of the powerful Florentine family. The Medici, who lived very near the church, entrusted Filippo Brunelleschi with restructuring the already ageing building. Thus, the great architect began work on the so-called Old Sacristy, which was completed in 1428, and then turned to construction of the Basilica which, after his death in 1446, was completed by Antonio Manetti, his pupil, heir and biographer.

In 1523 Pope Clement VII (Giulio de' Medici) charged Michelangelo with the task of transforming the buildings surrounding the cloister into a library (the so-called Medici-Laurentian Library). Michelangelo's design was brought to full completion only in 1568 by his pupils Vasari and Ammannati.

In 1520 the Pope had also entrusted Michelangelo with construction of a New Sacristy in portions of the building behind the apse of the Basilica, where, as in Brunelleschi's Sacristy, the tombs of the most celebrated of the Medici family were to be placed. Michelangelo oversaw the construction of this complex structure, which was nearly finished by 1534, though its actual completion had to wait until 1554-1555 under the supervision of Vasari and Ammannati.

In the early 17th Century Giovanni de' Medici had the idea of adding the family Mausoleum to the large area between the Basilica and Michelangelo's New Sacristy, and his design was carried out by Nigetti (1602). The complexity of the new structure and the dazzling semi-precious stone mosaic decoration made the work arduous and the crypt's completion dragged on for decades. It received new impetus in the 18th Century thanks to Anna Maria Luisa de' Medici, the Palatine Elector and last of the Medici line, who engaged the architects Giuseppe and Ferdinando Ruggieri to design and build the cupola that was to be a reduced version of that covering the church of Santa Maria del Fiore. With the extinction of the Medici family line and the advent of the Lorraine, the building remained partially incomplete, although the work of finishing the interior actually continued up until the 1960s. As this Medici Mausoleum is beyond the scope of our current interests, we shall forego a detailed explanation of its art and significance.

The whole sepulchral complex, including the two funeral chapels and the crypt, was separated from the church of San Lorenzo in 1855, when the square of Piazza di Madonna Aldobrandini was remodelled in order to provide an independent entrance and a wholly new artistic course beginning with the Crypt and ending with

Michelangelo's New Sacristy. Although it became a museum in its own right, it nevertheless remains inextricably linked to San Lorenzo by the often visionary qualities that characterise this extraordinary historical and artistic unit.

Last in this brief overview of the Basilica's history is the question of the façade, still missing to this day. The project was entrusted to Michelangelo, who designed it and made a number of models, but was forced to interrupt the work in 1520, when the contract was rescinded.

Often over the course of the following centuries, especially in 17th Century, it was thought to give an 'official face' to that which is perhaps the most famous church in Florence. Numerous designs were made, such as those by Poccianti and Bazzani. However, after much and at times dangerous vacillation, the splendid building was fortunately left as it is, with its naked, enigmatic face, almost as if none dared compromise the wonders hidden from sight within.

Therefore, together, this never-realised façade (models of which are however left to us), the Library and the New Sacristy constitute the only architectural complex in Florence wholly designed by Michelangelo and the absolutely only one whose construction, as it was completed during his lifetime, he was able to oversee even in the finishing details carried out by his pupils.

Therefore, let us begin with the Medici-Laurentian Library, today an Institute of the Ministero per i Beni Culturali (Ministry for Arts and Culture), which holds what is undoubtedly Italy's and one of the world's greatest collections of ancient codes and manuscripts (outside the Vatican Library) and whose core is constituted by the entire library of the Medici dynasty, the vastest and most celebrated in the Renaissance world.

As already mentioned, it was the Medici pope, Clement VII, who in 1525 decided to gather the entire family library within the walls of San Lorenzo. He charged Michelangelo with designing the spaces within which to store and consult the vast amount of scholarly material.

As Antonio Paolucci notes, just as the Uffizi was the prototype for future art galleries, so was the Medici-Laurentian Library "the archetype of all libraries. It is unlikely that there exists anywhere in the world a 16th-century atmosphere that has conserved such a high level of excellence and equally great formal homogeneity." (A. Paolucci, *The Museum of the Medici Chapels and San Lorenzo,* Livorno 1999, p. 44).

Michelangelo thus planned out the entire library (the Vestibule and Reading Room) from 1523 until 1534, the year he moved to Rome. From then up to 1568, its construction was supervised and completed by Vasari and Ammannati, who adhered strictly to their Maestro's designs.

Opposite page:
Vestibule of the
Medici-Laurentian
Library

The Vestibule of the library defines Michelangelo's unique, truly dramatic conception of architecture as realised through its tight dialectical relationship to the space containing it. In the relatively limited area developed in the vertical, Michelangelo defines enormous,

complex structures – the three-tiered walls with false windows, the colonnades, pilasters and tension rods – that engulf all who enter in a space that extends before one's eyes like a truly malleable substance, a substance that, through the structure's signs and symbols acquires the value of high functionality.

The triple staircase is closed in the centre between the two lateral flights free at their sides, but linked to the back wall through a true architectural mainspring coil. Each and every step of the central flight, carried out by Buontalenti, is a portion of space under development, hewn from the space of the whole Vestibule. The staircase is made of dark *pietra serena* stone, as are all the more tensed structures in the room, and is visually wedged within the limits of the Reading Room visible through the door beyond, an effect enhanced by the thrust of the coils bounding the two lateral flights of stairs.

The Reading Room then opens immediately above the stairs to contain the propellant strength of the Vestibule and closes it in an ultimate tier marked by the repeating architectural forms that at

Above:
Bartolomeo Ammannati, Staircase leading to the Library, 1559

Opposite page:
Reading Room of the Medici-Laurentian Library

the time gave new meaning to the age-old Florentine conception of "central-focus" perspective. Here, each and every particular, from the benches to the showcases and blazons, was designed by Michelangelo, the single exception being the splendid red and yellow terracotta floor by his pupil "il Tribolo", probably following an idea by Michelangelo, as can be inferred from the presence of the same geometric forms found throughout the entire complex.

Based therefore on this perfect duality – tension and expansion in action – the Library represents a true paradigm that must be understood in order to grasp the greater 'ideal' and 'mechanical' complexity of the subsequent New Sacristy.

In reality the two environments, though separated in the museum's current layout, are inextricably linked. Rather, one could say, with perhaps excessively explicatory hyperbole, that the Library and the New Sacristy are set in dialectic counterpoint to the interior space of San Lorenzo and the Old Sacristy. The two sacristies present the same unifying, harmonious plan, and the dependencies between them are further accentuated by the same relationship existing between the cupola of each and its bearing walls.

But contrary to the perfect harmony and proportionality of Brunelleschi's execution, Michelangelo almost causes the ancient metre to burst through his very choice of the powerful structural frame in dark *pietra serena* (as in the Library), tensed in an ascensional motion as far as the oculus of the dome.

This principal framework is then counterbalanced by all the other element-forces present within the space, elements whose

intensities vary with changes in lighting, especially where the dense, splendid sculpting is charged by the tension of the yellow-rose colours, transparency effects and reflecting white of the plaster.

Below, the black and white floor marks similar patterns and joins in imparting a sense of tension, establishing itself as the origin of the unifying mesh.

The development upwards presupposes an evident dialectic relationship referring to the 'low' structures and mosaic of the pavement that maintain this ascensional tendency in constant motion. Thus, one can understand how such an architectural system is said, not to merely 'represent', but to be equated with the idea of liberation of the captive body toward the spheres of the spirit, and is at once a demonstration of the impossibility of separating the two elements – body and spirit – whose eternal cycle defines

Preceding page:
Cupola of the New
Sacristy

Above and opposite
page:
New Sacristy

44

the whole of humanity and realises the mystery of the immortality of the individual soul.

The impact of this environment on the first-time observer is therefore a once-in-a-lifetime experience. Even more than the enormous spaces of the Sistine Chapel, here one feels driven by a formal and spiritual will able to make us perceive something 'visible', something that manages to move our senses and minds through an aesthetic path, that is at the same time both spiritual and liberating. The structure's lowest level, marked by the squared-off pilasters, capitals and trabeations, bears the two Medici tombs, one facing the other: that of Lorenzo, duke of Urbino, at whose feet are

Below:
New Sacristy with the
*Madonna and Child
between Saints
Cosmas and Damian*

Opposite page:
Madonna and Child,
detail

Dawn and *Dusk*, and that of Giuliano, duke of Nemours with *Day* and *Night*. The wall between the two tombs holds an apsidiole – a smaller version of Brunelleschi's apse – containing an altar within a space whose greater illumination is reflected on the opposite, completely plastered wall. This latter wall is the only one not wholly panelled in marble. Its lower border is a marble plinth containing the mortal remains of Giuliano de Medici and Lorenzo il Magnifico, which were moved here in 1559 from their temporary burial sites in the Old Sacristy.

Above the plinth, in a particularly bright area due the light reflected by the white of the plaster, are three statues: Michelangelo's *Madonna and Child*, flanked by *Saints Cosmas and Damian*, patron saints of the Medici, by two of Michelangelo's followers, Montorsoli and Raffaello da Montelupo, respectively, perhaps after a design by their Maestro, judging by the main stylistic elements.

The *Madonna and Child* was sculpted in 1521, therefore at the early stages of Michelangelo's planning of the Chapel, as if the artist, in defining this high "place of the soul and the body" still wished to recall the original theme of Divine Procreation. This Madonna, seemingly rising from the two material steps sustaining her, unfolds in a growing serpentine course, which is transformed into a dynamic space gathering in the body of Child Jesus, turned toward the mother in a coupling of structural forces that would be a paradigm for innumerable painters and sculptors during the

16th and 17th Centuries. Maria's exquisite head rises in an unprecedented flux above this structural node (defining as well the course of the major viewing perspective to the viewer's left), almost absorbing her Child's face in its features, divinely delineated in the porous marble. Surveying the entire setting, her gaze is poised as the point of emotional convergence, directly mirroring the Crucifix on the altar opposite.

On either side of this intense 'Epiphany zone', the thickening of the marble statues and the dark stone delineate the area of the 'material world', within which are set the two major tombs, char-

Tomb of Giuliano de' Medici, duke of Nemours

48

acterised by the symbols of time personified: *Dawn, Dusk, Day* and *Night*. Apart from the passage of time, the distinctive poses of the two character-heroes symbolise Man's dual nature, in that they have been consigned to immortality by the artistic act in the precise moments exalting their attributes of *action* and *thought*.

The foregoing synopsis of the Florentine neo-platonic ideas adhered to by the sculptor in those years is not only necessary to an understanding of the singularity of such works, it also serves to transform the programmatic rhetorical potential of Michelangelo's unique and sublime style. That is to say, these symbolic fig-

Tomb of Lorenzo de' Medici, duke of Urbino

49

ures attain their truly universal significance through a formal elaboration whose meaning lies, not in the highly skilled execution so common up to the end of the 15th Century, but in the meaning recovered from the unrepeatable actions of the individual in all its uniqueness, a process thereby akin to divine creativeness.

No other work can better help us understand this precise way of reasoning, which was to become the patrimony of artistic thought and philosophy up to and beyond the aesthetics of romanticism. Let us then return to our reading of these masterpieces. The three walls containing the two main tombs is completely faced with marble and *pietra serena* – both of which have the ability to give

Above:
Night, detail

Opposite page:
Dawn, detail

off a 'natural colouring' within the abstractness of the rest of the architecture. These, close off and enhance the architectural elements (frames, cornices, false windows, tympani, pilasters), thus establishing the metre of the spaces within which each of the monuments is situated. Within the opening demarcated by the dark pilasters (on the other two walls analogous pilasters surround the altar on one side and the tombs of Lorenzo and Giuliano on the other), Michelangelo creates true architecture, a sort of complex trisected façade overhung by plaques and festoons. In the deep central opening on each side are set the seated figures of the Heroes, each calibrated in a space that just barely contains it – just large enough to allow the architectural framing to allow some elements to emerge and thereby propel the dialectical relationship between space and figure. The urn below each statue, arched as the tympani of the two false windows, sustains the two symbolic figures that seem to push the limits of the two sides framing them. In this design, which equates architectural space with sculptural

space, Michelangelo re-establishes the relationship already set forth in the two 'orders' of the Medici-Laurentian Library. The tension in the underlying marble group, built on arched 'coil' motifs, just as in the library staircase, is directed onto the 'ordered' structure of the walls with the niche containing the Heroes' images. From an emotional representation of the 'material world' thus begins that formal process of ascension toward the sublime light of the Divine that Michelangelo wished to represent in the Sacristy.

It must be said that the reading provided here aims to give only a brief overview that cannot hope to exhaust the perfection and irrefutability of all the relationships amongst the various architectural elements and the sculptures themselves, relationships through which the *pathos* of the figures and their tormented histories unfolds.

Opposite page:
Portrait of Giuliano de' Medici, duke of Nemours

To the right:
Night, detail, *the owl*

In this complex system, on the right side, Giuliano de' Medici is depicted in a vigorous, alert posture, tensed on the axis formed by the sceptre in hand and the right leg with foot flexed, nearly in the act of rising. With his bare head and vivid, almost perturbed expression, he epitomises *Action* and, like his companion opposite, seems to divide the two symbols of time stretched before his feet, as a rock-cliff divides the force of the impinging wave.

These four symbols of time are perhaps Michelangelo's most beautiful and complex sculptures, clearly essential to the overall significance of the monuments, but just as meaningful and self-contained in their own individual right. Above the mortal remains of Giuliano and below his 'eternal' image, both *Night* and *Day* are

Tomb of Giuliano de' Medici, *Night*

powers generating true substance within the attractive forces of the architecture, a substance in itself autonomous, but yet 'containing' the symbolic sense.

The need to widely vary one's point of viewing and the possibility of reading the sculptures individually in the space that they themselves determine offer a series of interpretative readings rich in sudden pauses, references and attractive forces that no other statue, even the splendid programmatic experiments of Bernini, have been able to attain.

The serpentine course of both the figures (*Day* and *Night*) reveals the inner torsion, the almost visionary accentuation of details and a level of finishing that sparks lunar reflections over the polished

Tomb of Giuliano de' Medici, *Day*

Opposite page:
Portrait of Lorenzo
de' Medici, duke of
Urbino

Below:
Dusk, detail

surfaces of *Night* and defines strong contrasts on the limbs of *Day*, whose so-called "not-finished" face elicits a near dazzling sensation, further stressing the different atmosphere surrounding the head of *Night*, hidden in shadow. The replication of the posture (*Night* opening from its left, *Day* closing from its right) define a tightly linked succession that further enhances the inner relationships of their bodies.

The two dichotomous symbols (Day-Night) are worthy allegories for the 'active temperament', epitomised by Giuliano, while *Dawn* and *Dusk*, intermediary phases in the sun's course, are more suited to the 'contemplative temperament' that is symbolised by the figure of Lorenzo. This latter, (traditionally called the "thinker") is represented in full armour with head resting on his left hand in a meditative pose. The right leg, contrary to that of Giuliano, is in a resting position and delineates the exact axis of the nude reclining figure of *Dawn*, almost as if to recall the illuminating powers of thought. This structural continuity, absent as we have seen in the previous group, also defines another axis, beginning with the Hero's head, which is turned to regard the bent figure of *Twilight* (while *Dawn* is emergent, imbued with gathering strength), through a line of force that dissipates its energy through the strong resolution of the crossed leg.

Thus, the 'earthly level' of the representation ceases and gives rise

to two other, ever more luminous architectural levels, more rarefied and reiterative through the curves of the arches and joints of the pilasters, which stretch skyward towards the stark light of the dome. Here, absolute spirit is represented by the white of the plaster and the study of the light filtering through the central oculus.

For the sake of clar-

ity, this reading has only addressed the main point of view from which, according to Michelangelo's intent, these single masterpieces can be regarded and understood, and through which one can appreciate their unique relationship to the architecture containing them. However, as already mentioned, to fully appreciate these masterpieces, one must keep in mind the existence of the myriad variations, not only foreseen by Michelangelo to the very last detail, but born of his unprecedented conception of space as a concrete element indivisible from 'substance'. For this reason, the eye (and accordingly, the mind) follows an uninterrupted course that develops specific variants, each bearing its own specific meaning.

Therefore, this flowing perspective also clarifies the unusual relationship that the sculptor creates between the expansive breadth of the four symbolic statues and their points of support, formal-

Tomb of Lorenzo de' Medici, *Dusk*

ly solid, but dynamically precarious, onto which they bear down from above on the volute springs of the sarcophagi, protruding laterally by almost a meter. This gives rise to true visual motion, by which the plinths do not statically uphold the figures, but are moving bases, expanding continuously within the 'cosmic' movement on which the whole complex is built. This illustrative path through one of the consummate masterpieces ever conceived of by man risks distracting the viewer from appreciating all the myriad decorative details distributed throughout the main architectural elements and the monuments themselves. Each and every particular of this complex, down to the decorative bands and candelabra, was designed, and many even executed, by Michelangelo himself, who measured the minutest detail, normally relegated secondary status, by the same exacting standards as the crucial elements of his work.

Tomb of Lorenzo de' Medici, *Dawn*

The Cathedral *Pietà*

Last in this adventurous trip through the Florence of Michelangelo is the *Pietà*, one of the artist's last works, until recently kept in the church of Santa Maria del Fiore and now in the Museum of the Opera del Duomo. This work was performed in Rome between 1550 and 1555, immediately before or during the same period as the so-called *Rondanini Pietà*. According to Vasari the sculptor, by then exercising his art for himself alone, in the attempt to resolve his enormous existential restlessness (and he was then absolutely free from the need to respect conventions), intentionally mutilated this monument and left it incomplete. The figure of Mary Magdalen was later poorly completed by Tiberio Calcagni, and the sculpture was brought to Florence in the mid 17th Century.

Together with the *Rondanini Pietà* and *Palestrina Pietà*, it represents the last, arduous stage in the development of Michelangelo's language at its most expressive potential. The working of the material is accentuated in a sort of baring of the stone to make it, as was once said, "the mirror of the soul" – to make it better able to transcribe, beyond all rules of tradition, the emotions and thoughts of a form that, once the senses of the body's material and in its relationship to the spirit were thoroughly explored, could now overcome the material itself, requiring of the marble solely to represent the idea.

Over the *Pietà* looms the hooded countenance of Michelangelo himself, who in the guise of Joseph of Arimathea supports Christ and the Virgin, whose limbs seem to crumble, either in the light or in a sort of physical abandonment. The figure of Christ therefore falls immobile in that painful, total spirituality that must be said, beyond any rhetorical excess, fully invests the subsequent *Rondanini Pietà*.

The assertive artist that had created the new and triumphant universe of *David*, *Bacchus*, and the *Doni Tondo* ends his artistic course by representing solely the visions of his own consciousness and thus formally introduces sculpture to centuries and centuries of history.

Opposite page:
Pietà, 1550-1555

Michelangelo's drawings

The Gabinetto di Disegni e Stampe (Drawing and Print Office) of the Uffizi, located in the Museum of Casa Buonarroti, holds nearly two hundred of Michelangelo's drawings – inventive designs and sketches fundamental to an understanding of the artist's career. In fact, it was on many of Michelangelo's drawings found here that Varsari based his subsequent elaboration of the supremacy of painting.

However, as these drawings represent an historic patrimony conserved within the collections to which they belong, and therefore not open to public viewing, they shall not be addressed in detail, a task that would in any event prove far too lengthy for the purposes of this book.

Chronology

1475 Michelangelo Buonarroti is born in Caprese to Lodovico di Leonardo di Buonarroto Simoni and Francesca di Neri di Miniato del Sera. After moving to Settignano, Michelangelo is entrusted to a nursemaid, daughter and wife of stonemasons – an event that the artist would judge as a determining factor in his formation.

1488 After long forbiddance, Michelangelo's father sends him to the Florentine workshop of the painters Domenico and Davide Ghirlandaio, which however the young apprentice abandons before the agreed upon term of three years.

1489-1492 In the following years Michelangelo prefers to frequent the Medici gardens of San Marco where, under the guidance of Bertoldo di Giovanni, he studies ancient sculpture. His first endeavours arouse the admiration of Lorenzo il Magnifico who, treating him "not differently from a son", welcomes him to court, where Michelangelo would spend much time with Poliziano and the other humanists of the Medici entourage, assimilating the platonic doctrines they adhered to (which were to become a fundamental element in both his artistic and poetic activities).

1490-1492 He performs his first sketches (based on frescoes by Giotto and Masaccio) and the reliefs of the *Madonna of the Steps* and the *Battle of the Centaurs*.

1494-1496 Perturbed by the political events following the death of Lorenzo, Michelangelo flees Florence and spends one year in Bologna. His departure for Rome marks the beginning of a decade of intense and fortunate activity, during which Michelangelo asserts himself as one of the greatest artists of the time, sculpting the *Vatican Pietà*, amongst other works.

1501-1505 Michelangelo returns to Florence and executes the *Pitti Tondo*, the *Taddei Tondo*, the *Madonna and Child* (today in Bruges) and *David*, which was placed before the entrance of Palazzo della Signoria.

1505-1506 The artist returns to Rome where Pope Julius II entrusts him with execution of his grandiose sepulchral monument. Michelangelo, after having designed an imposing architectural and sculptural complex – celebrating the triumph of the Church more than that of the pontiff – once again leaves the city, indignant over the indifference of the Pope, who had in the meantime turned his attention to Bramante's plans for the new St. Peter's Basilica. Back in Florence he takes up work on the *Battle of Cascina* and *Saint Matthew*.

1508 Michelangelo accepts a contract to decorate the Sistine Chapel vault and completes the fresco series over four years of tireless, solitary labour.

1513 After the death of Julius II, the artist signs a second contract for the pontiff's sepulchral monument, a project also destined to an unhappy fate. Only in 1545 would the last version of the work finally come to be placed in San Pietro in Vincoli in Rome, thus concluding the long and painful episode that Michelangelo himself would define as "the tragedy of the sepulture".

1516-1520 The Medici pope, Leo X commissions the façade of San Lorenzo in Florence from Michelangelo. However, the contract is rescinded in 1520 and Michelangelo, with great resentment, begins construction of the New Sacristy and the Medici-Laurentian Library.

1527 Following the Sack of Rome and the expulsion of the Medici from Florence, Michelangelo is named "governor and overseer of the building and fortification of the city walls" and actively participates in the defence of the city besieged by papal and imperial troops.

1530-1534 With the fall of the Florentine Republic, only the pardon of Clement VII saves Michelangelo from the revenge of the Medici and their followers. He once again takes up work on the New Sacristy and the Tomb of Julius II. In these years he sculpts the four *Prisoners* and *Apollo*.

1534 Michelangelo definitively leaves Florence and settles in Rome.

1536-1541 He accepts the papal commission to fresco the altar wall of the Sistine Chapel with the *Last Judgement*.

1550-1564 During these, his last years, Michelangelo's interests turn especially to architecture: the Medici-Laurentian Library, the layout of the square of Piazza del Campidoglio in Rome and his work on the new Vatican Basilica. He sculpts the *Palestrina Pietà* , the *Pietà* of the Florentine Cathedral and the *Rondanini Pietà*.

1564 Michelangelo dies in his house in Rome on February 18 at the age of nearly ninety. By the express will of the artist himself, his nephew has the corpse secretly transported to Florence to be buried in Santa Croce.